VIRTUALLY THERE

Dos and Don'ts for Planning, Chairing,
and Holding Virtual Board
and Annual General Meetings

DR. DEBRA L. BROWN,
ROB DEROOY,
AND
JAKE SKINNER

VIRTUALLY THERE

Dos and Don'ts for Planning, Chairing,
and Holding Virtual Board
and Annual General Meetings

DR. DEBRA L. BROWN,
ROB DEROOY,
AND
JAKE SKINNER

ethos
collective

Printed in the United States of America

Published by Ethos Collective™
PO Box 43, Powell, OH 43065
www.ethoscollective.vip

ISBN: 978-1-63680-044-8 (Paperback)
ISBN: 978-1-63680-046-2 (Ebook)

Available in paperback and e-book

Any Internet addresses (websites, blogs, etc.) and telephone numbers printed in this book are offered as a resource. They are not intended in any way to be or imply an endorsement by Ethos Collective™, nor does Ethos Collective™ vouch for the content of these sites and numbers for the life of this book.

Some names and identifying details have been changed to protect the privacy of individuals.

Praise for *Virtually There*

"With the dramatic shift to virtual board meetings and AGMs, and the positive impact many are seeing on director collaboration, attendance and inclusivity, there could hardly be a better moment for hands-on, cutting-edge guidance on how to make the most of these important events in corporate life. The world-leading experts at Governance Solutions have given us a practical tool for success and their new book earns a place on the desk of governance professionals everywhere."

Brenda Sweeney, APR, FCPRS, C.Dir. Independent Director | Reputation & Risk Expert

"Virtually There is an excellent resource for virtual board and AGM meetings, which I highly recommend! The book is well-written and very practical. It offers practical tips and guidance to help boards chairs, executives, and governance professionals understand the challenges and opportunities in running an effective mission critical board and annual general meetings virtually."

James W. Metcalf, COO, Canadian Centre for Christian Charities

More Governance Resources to Help You and Your Board

Earn Your Professional Director® (Pro.Dir®) Designation

The Professional Director Education and Certification Program® is a world-class, **online director education program** where you can build competence and confidence in governance while you earn a Pro.Dir® designation. Whether you work for a small company or a Fortune 500 enterprise; are a board member, senior executive, or provide support to a board; serve in the private, public, or not-for-profit sector; have a little, some, or a lot of governance experience; this program will build the confidence, skills, knowledge, and competence in governance you need to make it in today's complex boardroom. professionaldirector.com

Evaluate Your Board and Chief Executive Officer (CEO)

The Board Evaluation Solution is a best practice, comprehensive, **online board evaluation suite** that is second to none! Leveraging our many years of board evaluation experience, this suite lets you easily and clearly identify areas for action and improvement. You can select evaluation of the board, its committees, the board and committee chairs, and individual director peer and self-evaluations—or any combination of these! All reports give you comprehensive results and benchmarked scorecards in key dimensions of board effectiveness. governancesolutions.ca

The CEO Evaluation Solution is an online CEO evaluation tool that makes this task as easy as 1, 2, 3! Get confidential, objective, professional results. Our tool evaluates the CEO in three distinct ways: against accountabilities; against the results and outcomes of goals, objectives, and targets; and against their leadership qualities. governancesolutions.ca

Optimize Your Governance

Governance Consulting and Coaching will propel and optimize your governance effectiveness and lead to superior corporate results. You can expect clear outcomes, objective assessment, helpful advice, and actionable strategies. Whether you need a comprehensive governance review, one-on-one coaching in governance skills, team coaching to enhance board solidarity, or help with that difficult director, our consultants can be trusted to be discreet, sensitive, and practical. governancesolutions.ca

Organize with Your Board Portal

BoardConnex® is the latest in board portal solutions provided by the savvy technology team of Sandbox Software Solutions and the governance experts at Governance Solutions. This secure, web-based online board portal makes it easy and convenient for you to oversee your organization with confidence. Integrate governance resources, advice, and collaboration tools with meeting and document management! boardconnex.com

Contact us today! contact@governancesolutions.ca

Dedicated to all who meet every day!

With special thanks to our editor Lorna Stuber and those on the Governance Solutions team who made this book possible: David A. H. Brown, Vicki Dickson, Alex Martin, Rafael Mazotine, and Dave McComiskey.

CONTENTS

INTRODUCTION

Virtual meetings done well and with intention mean that you can be *Virtually There!*

Virtually There: Dos and Don'ts for Planning, Chairing, and Holding Virtual Board and Annual General Meetings is based on a series of online learning events developed and delivered in the spring of 2020, during the immediate throes of the COVID-19 pandemic when in-person meetings were impossible.

These scary times have challenged boards around the world. An unexpected positive outcome of restricted travel is that virtual board meetings and annual general meetings (AGMs) have, in many cases, been surprisingly successful. With no travel required and easy access, these virtual meetings have allowed more people to attend and take part in the annual reflection on the life of the organization.

Living and leading through a global pandemic has taught us all a few things, including how to use technology to meet virtually. For many boards, virtual meetings will continue to be the norm; in fact, some may choose not to meet in person again as a matter of preference, efficiency, and cost savings. Whether you have already made that decision or are weighing the pros and cons of meeting online versus in person, *Virtually There* provides insights and practical tips on how to make the most of these important online gatherings.

CHAPTER 1

WHY MEET?

Meetings are made for change.

Whether there are two people in the meeting or two thousand, we meet so that we can create change.

> **Meetings are made for change.**

Meetings drive innovation and growth.

The more we interact around important issues, the more *iron sharpens iron,* and we innovate. When we innovate, growth quickly follows.

Meetings facilitate communication and decision-making. Communication is central to every area of life and business. Clarity in our communications drives our personal growth, understanding, and development and propels the health and depth of our relationships, both personal and corporate, while making decisions that affect the management of our lives and businesses.

That's why we meet.

There are several methods and modes of communication, none more effective than person-to-person interaction. When COVID-19 hit the world in early 2020, suddenly, in-person meetings stopped. And yet, if there was ever a time when people needed to meet, to make decisions, to drive innovation and growth, to make change, it was in the throes of a global emergency.

The pivot to virtual meetings was swift and welcome. The learning curve for some was just as swift and welcome. For others it was painful and remains an unwelcome approach, a hindrance to effective interaction.

> **The pivot to virtual meetings was swift and welcome.**

Virtual meetings are here to stay. The good news is, virtual meetings can be just as effective, and dare I say it, even more so, than those at which people are physically present.

This book is intended to help you take some practical steps that will make your virtual board meetings and AGMs effective and efficient.

In the traditional meeting cycle for board meetings and AGMs, we generally take eight steps to complete the cycle; six of those steps happen before the meeting ever starts. This cycle should not be different for virtual meetings. We still need to instigate change and make decisions; we need to communicate, innovate, and grow, regardless of whether we meet in a physical meeting room or a virtual one.

In these times when health and safety concerns lead us to meet virtually and technology has progressed to support this in effective ways, the face of our meetings has changed. Regardless of new approaches to meeting, the basic organizational structures and etiquettes remain unchanged in their fundamentals.

The purpose of any given meeting may be varied, yet all include aspects of these elements: informing and educating;

influencing, motivating, directing, and leading; meeting needs; accomplishing objectives and goals; empowering board and staff members and fostering teamwork; reaching conclusions and making decisions; and responding to the meeting outcomes by making change.

The degree of achievement and success in any meeting will be based on two main factors of equal importance: firstly, the communicator or leader needs to be able to positively and effectively *communicate*, and secondly, the organizer(s) of the meeting must be highly proficient in the planning and follow-up of every detail.

Every participant in any given meeting must both bring with them and take away something of value to them. Perhaps, for attendees, the value of the meeting is in the knowledge they have shared or newly acquired: a fresh perspective, a renewed commitment, a newfound sense of empowerment, or simply the feeling that they have contributed to the overall success of the meeting. The measure of success placed on the gathering by the individuals involved, whether chair, participant, planner, or communicator, will be the knowledge that has been gained either individually or as a collective.

> Every participant in any given meeting must both bring with them and take away something of value to them.

A poorly planned meeting has dramatic costs attached, the least of those being financial. Obviously, the financial costs can be significant, yet the larger costs are found in stalled momentum, indecision, and poor morale, as well as the irresponsible handling of precious human resources, failed communications, and in the squandering of unrecoverable

> A poorly planned meeting has dramatic costs attached, the least of those being financial.

time and energy. As if this is not enough to lose, the most significant waste of all these is the loss of opportunity.

The successful, well-planned, and well-executed meeting fully acknowledges and takes complete advantage of the opportunity to communicate and accomplish in creative and innovative ways. When meetings are approached in this manner, the resulting change and growth will be in proportions that far exceed financial measures.

7 Key Principles

There are only seven basic principles you need to follow to hold a successful, productive board meeting or AGM, virtual or otherwise:

1. The purpose for your meeting must be beneficial for the organization and for *all* parties involved.

2. You must set specific desired outcomes for the meeting. These outcomes need to meet the *needs* of both the organization and the meeting participants.

3. Professionalism, planning, order of agenda items, and *attention to detail* will propel your meeting from being a good get-together to being one that drives productive change and builds momentum.

4. The location and suitability of the *place of meeting* will make or break the meeting! Your careful thought is imperative here. In the virtual environment, your choice of technology matters.

5. Your meeting should be *positive in tone, open to informed dialogue,* and *focused on outcomes.* The sharing of information should be enabled by an assortment of communicating methods, approaches,

visuals, and engagement techniques alternating throughout the meeting.

6. Attendee participation and *hands-on* or *experiential learning* create an atmosphere in which the most effective gains can be made.

7. Include an element of *evaluation following each meeting*. You should answer these questions:

Did we reach our outcomes in a positive and helpful manner?

Have our organizational needs been met?

Were our meeting participants engaged, informed, and respected? Did we gain and give value?

Did any lasting conclusions and decisions get reached because of the meeting?

Did the meeting spur innovation and action?

How could we change and improve our approach for our next meeting?

Is this a meeting I would want to attend, and would I pay for the privilege by investing my time or money to do so again in the future?

In the case of an AGM, your shareholder or member will attend your meeting because they have a vested personal interest in doing so. They may attend because they are curious, because they feel they must, or better yet, because they truly want to know more or to be involved with your organization. Regardless, they are at your meeting and they represent an opportunity for positive, effective communication resulting in continuous and lasting growth.

Your meeting has been planned. You have the attention of everyone present. Attendees are enthusiastically anticipating the meeting; they are prepared and ready and willing to listen and participate fully. Don't lose them now! Many meetings succeed, yet many more do not. The single common thread that can either weave its way through the event or tangle and break in the process is the ability to truly communicate and connect with the group around the purpose of the meeting.

CHAPTER 2
VIRTUAL AGM DOS AND DON'TS

A virtual meeting has the same objectives as an in-person meeting, but the virtual meeting has special requirements that need to be accommodated. Some new players to the team may need to ensure that all the technological components on their end function as required.

Before the Meeting

Assemble the Team

Consider having a team to assist in monitoring all the elements required in a virtual meeting. The quality of the internet connection for those team members is part of that decision. You'll want at least two people with separate internet connections leading the meeting just in case one person's internet goes down. It happens. And even without technological hiccups, a team approach will make your meeting progress more smoothly. For instance, having someone to just control slides, someone else who handles chat, and a third person who handles motions, especially if you have motions from the floor, will ensure that all of these roles are covered simultaneously. These team members need to be knowledgeable about AGM rules and legislative and regulatory rules as well as the bylaws and rules specific to your organization.

For example, you may accept motions from the floor and you may accept amendments to motions. In these cases, someone needs to keep track of motions and record them in writing. When it comes time to vote, you want motions written down rather than only having been presented verbally. You want to make sure everyone's voting on the same thing.

You may want someone for tech support—someone who's good with whatever applications you are using. You'll likely need more than one type of technology software to conduct a big AGM, depending on your voting. And you'll want someone in charge of registrations. Just as you would have if you held the AGM in your building, you need someone at the virtual door confirming attendees. Someone needs to be dedicated to recording shareholder attendance and to ensuring that people who shouldn't be in the room aren't.

You'll want someone dedicated to phone and email support. Before the meeting, for instance, there can be numerous emails or phone calls, even texts, about the meeting. Someone needs to respond to these queries. And during the meeting, someone needs to monitor any comments or questions from participants. For instance, if a shareholder indicates their audio isn't working, the meeting may need to be paused so that person can rectify the problem, or their contribution in the chat room may need to be allowed in the discussion since they cannot contribute verbally.

Some of these roles can be combined, but these tasks cannot all be left to the chair. While a moderator has a slightly different role than a chair, it is perfectly okay to have both. Assign different roles and tasks ahead of the meeting—whatever works to keep an orderly meeting and to make sure that questions are answered and other sidebars are dealt with as the meeting progresses.

Revise Rules for Virtual Process

In planning a virtual meeting, you'll need to make space and have processes in place to deal with attendee participation. Just like you would in an in-person meeting, you will want to have an orderly flow of communication, and typically the same rules about contact conduct will apply. But do review your normal rules, your procedural rules, and your parliamentarian rules to make sure they work in a virtual setting. For instance, there may be things that you do in person, such as raising a hand for comments or asking for a show of hands for votes, that you just can't do virtually. If you need to revise your rules or processes to adapt them to a virtual situation, make sure those revised rules are available to everyone in advance. And, if you've got a large group with thousands of attendees, you'll have to take a hard look at some of your processes to make sure they'll work virtually.

Ensure Your Member Information Is Up-to-date

Regardless of which platform you use, it is essential to the voting process to have an up-to-date member list with current contact information. Don't assume that a cell number you had on file from a year ago is still current. You want to be sure you're reaching your audience directly and as quickly as possible. A system such as ElectionBuddy is great because it can reach out via numerous methods, such as email or text. And when the opportunity for in-person meetings returns, you can use it to set up little polling stations.

Consider using the platform as a way to reach out to members before the meeting to confirm contact information and as the quickest and most reliable method of reaching them.

Anticipate Questions

Whenever you're having a meeting, especially an AGM, you want to anticipate questions so that you have a scripted response ready. Do some planning around this in advance of the meeting by understanding the concerns of your members or shareholders. In this way, you will be better able to address those issues and even answer those questions before they are asked. You will also streamline your process, as the same question won't be asked by multiple participants.

Select a Platform

Choose a platform that has the capability for simultaneous and instantaneous communication from attendees.

This doesn't mean everyone has their microphone open and can just blurt out questions and comments. With potentially hundreds of attendees at an AGM, that would be chaos! If everyone were able to speak at any time during the meeting, people would not be able to hear the presenters or each other. That's the opposite of instantaneous and available communication.

An efficient virtual meeting, like an in-person meeting, needs to provide time to work through the agenda but also to ensure it deals with the relevant topics and questions only. Off-topic questions can be tabled for another time. It is the role of the chair to ensure that the meeting—and its attendees—stay on topic. Allowing and encouraging attendee communication doesn't mean plunging into every rabbit hole that an attendee wants to pursue, especially when there can be hundreds of people in the meeting.

Get Familiar with the Software

Certainly, the leaders of your meeting need to have a good familiarity with the platforms you will use. You also want to do everything you can to prepare your attendees for using these platforms. Allow them to understand what technologies will be used and, if possible, let them use those platforms in advance, for example as a trial. The goal is to do whatever is possible everything possible in advance to reduce or ideally eliminate the amount of time people spend during the meeting trying to figure out how to get their video or audio on or how to use the voting system.

Whichever software platforms you select for your AGM, practice, practice, practice! Especially ensure that your chair, your moderator, and the people presenting are comfortable using it. You don't want these important participants to be encountering new software for the first time at the AGM! They need to know which software is being used, and they need to be comfortable with it. The last thing you need is a presenter who is not able to get their audio working or who does not know how to move a PowerPoint presentation forward. These kinds of glitches cause a meeting to grind to a halt. You'll lose engagement, and you'll lose your carefully planned timing.

Keep the Meeting Flowing

To conduct an AGM in any sector, it's important to consider how participants can interact—how they can ask questions, for instance. Communication with attendees is not optional.

A lot is going on in a virtual meeting, and technology is an even bigger part of a virtual meeting than it is at an in-person meeting. For instance, there's a chat room, presenters, motions, slide decks…and all of these tools rely on an internet connection. It is nearly impossible, and not recommended, for one person to juggle all of this alone.

Best Presentations

The meeting chair needs to establish and ensure clear roles for who's doing presentations. Those presentations need to be sharp and targeted, with simple slides. Presentations should be timed and scripted. In this way, there is less opportunity for a meeting to get sidetracked. Concise presentations—targeted and scripted—will also hold all attendees' attention.

Presenters too can use an extra set of hands or eyes. For instance, a presenter working from a script and keeping an eye on the time is not going to also be able to answer questions in the chat room. You may also want to consider having a presenter's slides available in advance. If, for instance, the presenter's internet goes down, the chair and chair's team will need to take over the session. As with any part of the virtual meeting, it makes good sense to have at least one other person working with the presenter to answer chat, for instance, or or provide tech support.

Visual Information

Attendees who are engaging in your virtual meeting will see a lot happening on their computer screens. There will be lots of faces of presenters, a chat going on the side, and there may also be a PowerPoint deck up. That is already a lot of visual interaction. To help attendees follow your presentation, don't use complicated slides or slides heavy with written content. You'll want to keep those slides visual, straightforward, and meaningful. As with any presentation, it's about talking to the slides, being succinct, staying on topic, and anticipating and answering questions as you go.

Votes and Polling

It is important to have at least one member of your team dedicated to polling and counting votes. And, it may not be the person who does this at in-person meetings. A virtual meeting with large numbers of shareholders or complicated votes requires a software solution with which your usual in-person vote-counter may not be familiar.

Many large, publicly-traded companies use a sophisticated platform like Lumi or Broadridge. These are expensive options designed specifically for large shareholder meetings. They are excellent platforms for organizations that can afford them and have skilled people to operate them. But for many organizations, they are simply out of reach financially.

Most of the popular virtual meeting platforms, such as Zoom or GoToMeeting, have basic polling options such as a simple *hands-up* function. Even with these systems, you are going to want another person to handle the polling because your virtual meeting will likely require several different platforms, such as your board portal app, your video conferencing system, and software for voting.

You'll need to be familiar with all the levels of software you're using. For example, a meeting may have Zoom for the actual board members and people who are interacting. And then for the larger audience, there may be a streaming service that may or may not allow interaction but instead provides a one-way view. By the time you're ready to roll with your meeting, you may be four levels deep into using different platforms!

Your organization may require proxy voting or weighted voting that these basic polling applications can't offer. In this case, you will need to consider having a secondary solution and the right team members to handle the voting. One platform that is flexible, user-friendly, and affordable is ElectionBuddy. Despite the friendly name, it offers serious security and integrity for the voting process.

The system allows for weighted voting and can accommodate a variety of voting styles. For example, it allows for fast opposing and cumulative scoring, and it does validate voting. A clear audit trail is critical to making sure that everyone involved is confident that the process is sound.

Polling is okay, but the use of a polling tool depends on what kind of vote you are having and whether your chosen approach is set up within your rules and bylaws as an allowed method of voting. Polling is limited, for instance, if you allow proxy voting. If someone's holding a bunch of proxies, polling won't handle it, and that's an issue.

Streamline Your Process

Registration

Just as it would if you had three hundred people coming to an in-person meeting, registration for a virtual meeting takes time. All three hundred people can't arrive at the starting time of the meeting. There needs to be time to get attendees through the registration process. Tell them in your notice of meeting that the meeting starts at a certain time but that they need to register before the meeting, and recommend they show up at least fifteen minutes in advance. Attendees need to be verified and confirmed. That takes time, and you don't want two hundred people in a waiting room at the time the meeting is supposed to start.

Staggered registrations can be a solution, but getting attendees to stick to that time structure can be challenging. It also depends on the size of your meeting. Staggering registration adds a lot of time to your process. For instance, doing half-hour windows with a large group can mean a long time in the waiting room for the ABC crowd as they wait for the XYZ group to arrive. Whichever process you choose, ensure that the process is crystal clear among the team members who are operating it.

Auto registration functionality is available with software from Broadridge or Lumi. With a system such as Zoom or Webex, you can restrict—and confirm—attendance to preregistered names and email addresses. This is useful for sessions where you need to confirm that certain people are *in the room* and others are not. Communicate to attendees ahead of time that they need to have a registered user account with an email address through Zoom or Webex before they join the meeting. Then the software will restrict the attendance to these users only. This approach can work to ensure that only the people you want in the meeting can access this stream. You might want to have a secondary stream that is more publicly available.

This way, your administrative team, or whoever is acting at the door as your *bouncer*, will have a member list and they have the registered email addresses to match names to.

Do a Dry Run

You want your team to be confident with the software that will be used for the AGM. Nothing wrecks a great presentation faster than technological incompetence. Consider a live run-through—a dress rehearsal—to ensure your administrative team and your presenters know how things work. For instance, have staff run through the registration process. A dry run ensures everyone has some practice with the role they've been given and that the AGM is not the first time they are working with the software in use.

How Long Should the Meeting Be?

It's difficult to offer an arbitrary time limit on the length of an AGM. In any meeting, there are standard issues that must be dealt with, such as presenting financials and discussing any changes to bylaws. But some years, the agenda may be more complex than others, for instance, if your organization has massive bylaw or other changes. As a target, try to limit the meeting to a two-hour maximum.

Keep in mind, you may have to change your bylaws to allow for a virtual AGM. If this is the case, then those changes have to be adopted at the AGM and you'd want to deal with that first.

Candidate Speeches

If candidates are making speeches, then they've got a presenter role and they should be scripted and tightly timed. Each candidate needs to have the same amount of time and running past that cannot be tolerated. They've got to understand that. So you want them, like any other presenter, to practice before the AGM with the software that will be used at the AGM.

Information for AGM participants, such as candidate profiles, can be distributed ahead of time. The method of distribution depends on your process for validating the information, but whatever process is used, organizers need to ensure that each candidate—with a speech or a bio—gets an equal opportunity.

Discourage Video Use for Non-board Members

In a small AGM, a video connection for all can be useful. For example, seeing twenty-five faces on your screen at a time is manageable. But having hundreds of participants on your screen can be simply distracting, and therefore you may want to limit video access to presenting members only.

Security

A virtual AGM needs to balance confidentiality and functionality. Where security is a priority, it may be preferable to use a platform that is more locked down. Webex, for instance, is a great platform with high security. Zoom, on the other hand, is a lot more user-friendly. It's easier to engage with a huge crowd in Zoom. However, there have been issues of security with Zoom, such as *Zoom-bombing*, where uninvited people can access your meeting. AGM organizers will need to mitigate these risks and weigh security concerns with accessibility; it's a trade-off.

Options such as GoToMeeting and GoToWebinar are also good options if you need to reach a mass audience. Their encryption levels aren't as high as other platforms such as Zoom, but if your organization is more familiar with these tools, they may be the better option. Your choice should always come down to weighing usability against confidentiality.

The platform doesn't matter if you're using a rural internet connection where simultaneous instantaneous interaction is impossible. It's incumbent upon the organization to put things in place that compensate for poor internet connectivity. For example, another option is using the conference line as a call-in option. Does the software platform you are using for your voting have a text-based voting system which will reach out to participants over text? With rural members, you can't always be a hundred percent sure that even the phone lines are going to work. It is a challenge.

In Camera Sessions

In camera sessions with or without the CEO rely on your ability to monitor and have strict control over who's on the call and who's off the call. In choosing a platform for your AGM, you need to look at this issue. How can you be assured that the people who need to leave the room do so? With something like Zoom, you've got a waiting room where those people can go. You would see them leave, and they wouldn't be able to get back in without coming back through the waiting room. Different platforms have different ways of holding people outside of a meeting.

Attendance

Virtual AGMs have not been popular in the past. Although their use is growing in the for-profit sector, in many organizations, proxy holders and special interest groups, in particular, don't like them. They think such meetings don't allow them input. Other people like them and say there's broader engagement because more people can get in. But to a large extent, the different opinions also have to do with your sector or organization.

Some organizations report better attendance at virtual AGMs than in-person ones. But attendance fluctuations in virtual or in-person meetings can also be attributed to the health of an organization. When things are going well, you have low attendance and when things are not going well, you have high attendance, regardless of how or where you meet.

CHAPTER 3
PLANNING A SUCCESSFUL VIRTUAL AGM

Organizations across the globe and in all sectors have postponed their AGMs during the pandemic as face-to-face meetings have not been possible. Now, months into this global challenge, many have realized the time has come to stop putting these off. There are matters that are both important and urgent, such as an auditor appointment and director elections, that must be addressed.

The Legal Right to Hold a Virtual AGM

Organizations planning to hold a virtual AGM need to first ensure they have the legal right to do so. Start by asking these three questions:

1. Have we checked legislation, regulation, and emergency measures regarding rights to hold a virtual AGM?

2. Do we need to amend our bylaws to hold a virtual AGM?

3. Have we got the right policy and protocols in place to hold a virtual AGM?

If your organization's bylaws do not explicitly allow a virtual AGM, there may be higher governing documents that will permit you to do so, or there may be an emergency act or legislation that allows for it. If there's nothing at the higher level, and your bylaws don't allow for it, then you can't have electronic meetings. The solution is for an organization to either change their meeting bylaws or find a higher authority to allow them to hold a virtual AGM.

In many instances, regulations and legislation don't anticipate fully electronic meetings. In most cases, organizations have written bylaws and rules of order with only in-person meetings in mind. Some bylaws will need to be amended or adapted to accommodate the virtual setting. Even if these changes are only temporary—to deal with an emergency for just one year—and even if there is a higher authority saying you can ignore a bylaw, these changes must be communicated effectively.

How to Ensure the Membership Is Confident in the Process

An AGM is generally a formal process where you're making some serious decisions. All the standard rights for the members that are in place for in-person meetings need to be protected in virtual meetings.

Debate is an important component of an AGM. The minority needs to be heard; individuals need to be able to express their views. A virtual meeting needs a process to confirm quorum so that you're protecting all the absentee members and ensuring a fair process. Your virtual meeting needs to have a suitable process for decision-making, ensuring that your rules of order can apply to virtual meetings. And, of course, how members will vote in a virtual meeting needs to be addressed. You will want to ensure that the same standards, bylaws, and processes for a legal, secure, and inclusive AGM are applied to electronic meetings as they are to in-person meetings.

Regional and Sectoral Differences

Different regions, like provinces or states, have different regulations. For instance, in Canada, an emergency regulation was put in place in the province of Ontario in 2020, along with a general state of emergency that was declared. The emergency regulation allows Ontario corporations to have virtual AGMs regardless of what their bylaws might say. Even if your bylaw is silent on this or prohibits electronic meetings, an emergency regulation such as this one allows you to go ahead anyway. Similar regulations or mandates were created for several other Canadian provinces through orders-in-council.

Several provinces had enabling legislation already in place that addressed electronic meetings. And this legislation all speaks to the issue of adequate communication. You still have to go to your bylaws to make sure virtual meetings are enabled there, too.

This creates a situation where a higher power has given you the authority to go forward. And it's given you the ability to do so without necessarily also changing your bylaws for the period during which the emergency orders are in place.

There are differences in emergency regulations from province to province.

Regulations also vary depending on whether you're a for-profit, a cooperative, a not-for-profit corporation, or a regulated industry. There can also be nuanced differences by industry within regions.

Here is another example from Canada. In the province of Saskatchewan, for most sectors, the government allows meetings by telephone, video conference, or electronic means, but that is still subject to the organization's articles or bylaws. The province hasn't permitted organizations to ignore the organization's articles or bylaws. Ultimately, Saskatchewan organizations whose bylaws prohibit electronic meetings needed to amend their bylaws in order to hold virtual meetings.

The *Canada Business Corporations Act* allows for federally incorporated organizations to hold virtual meetings.

Adequate Communication

The one thing all these regulations have in common is a proviso that the virtual meeting must allow shareholders and members to communicate adequately. Like many regulations, that gets defined once there's been some sort of a lawsuit or a common-law definition put to it. As yet, it hasn't yet been defined because it's never been through the courts. So *adequate communication* is poorly defined. Most organizations interpret *adequate communication* to refer to communication between the chair and the shareholders or members present and as a way for them to ask questions of each other. They don't necessarily need to be able to talk to each other as long as everyone can hear each other when they're asking questions or making motions.

Communicating Changes to Shareholders and Members

Your organization should not assume that your shareholders and members know about the legal rights or the legal hierarchy in terms of your ability to hold an AGM. The onus is on you when you're sending out your notice to shareholders or members to be clear about the authority under which you are calling this AGM. For instance, is it under an emergency regulation, an order-in-council, or the power of your bylaws? And will you be asking the members to pass a resolution at the AGM itself to put a standing rule in place? This must be determined ahead of time and then clearly communicated in your notice and also at the beginning of the meeting.

Unpacking the Legal Hierarchy of Governance

The highest form of written law is *statute law*. Statue laws are the acts that are passed by a state, province, or federal government. For every act, regulations are approved by the minister or governor responsible for that act. These regulations are rules that interpret the act and which you need to follow in order to be in compliance with the act. This is why, for example, through an emergency order, the government can tell organizations that they don't have to follow their bylaws in cases such as the COVID-19 shutdowns. Using our Ontario example, the emergency measure is an act of the Ontario legislature that gives the provincial government the power to put into effect an emergency regulation which overrides your bylaws.

If you want to hold a virtual board meeting, committee meeting, or AGM, first take a look at your own statutes and regulations as they may trump whatever is in your bylaws. Then go to your organization's bylaws, which are typically approved by your shareholders or members. There are hard and fast rules that must be consistent with your relevant act. Underneath your bylaws are the rules of order by which meetings are governed. For example, your bylaws may say that your meetings will be governed under *Robert's Rules of Order*, or your bylaws may be silent on that. Either way, it's up to the meeting members or the board to propose what rules of order you're going to adopt and follow.

Higher still in the governance hierarchy are standing rules or special rules. Standing rules are special and are essentially higher than rules of order. Here's an example of a special rule:

An organization was planning a virtual AGM and trying to decide how much time the meeting would need. They realized that if they gave everybody ten minutes to speak to every motion that was on the floor, as their rules of order allowed for, they would be there all day and all evening. Instead, at the beginning of the AGM, they passed a special rule for the governing of that virtual AGM which stipulated that for this meeting only, people will only have two minutes to speak to a motion and candidates will only have one minute to make their presentation. In this way, the organization was able to manage the meeting practically.

So, just as regulations can trump your bylaws, your organization has its own levels of internal hierarchy.

Standing Rules

Standing rules exist when the meeting adopts a specific set of rules of order. These are usually more than the generic rules of order in a standard book, for example. In terms of standing rules for your virtual meeting, you'll want to confirm that you have set and achieved agreement on the rules and processes for the meeting. And you'll need to ask yourself if there is additional information you need to send out to attendees, with or after your notice about procedures or processes, that may be different because you are meeting electronically.

In some cases, an organization will now have two sets of standing rules—the existing set for in-person meetings and a new one created exclusively for electronic meetings. This is because each environment requires different rules, and standing rules are important to an organization. Your shareholders and members must be on board with this; you need to have buy-in. If you don't have buy-in, if you don't have adapted standing rules, you have set yourself up for a chaotic and confusing meeting. Shareholders and members can challenge everything being done at a virtual meeting.

Having rules in place and ensuring attendees are aware of and understand those rules are important parts of your planning process. The goal is to have clarity and to ensure everybody is on the same page.

Consider that *Robert's Rules of Order* was originally written in 1876. There have of course been updates since then, but it's unlikely that anyone at that time was anticipating electronic meetings! So, you know there will be limitations to applying some of those rules to electronic meetings.

You will need to consider that any rule changes for virtual meetings can also be accommodated by your choice of meeting platform. For example, some technologies allow you to put your hand up virtually. Some don't. Some have chat; some have polling. You need to thoroughly understand the technology you're using so you can then adjust your normal standing rules to fit with the platform you're using. And importantly, any adjustments you make and the reasons for those adjustments need to be communicated with the membership; members need to understand the reasons for any rule changes.

Tech Solutions

Your organization, depending on its size, will likely need several layers of technologies. For instance, you're going to need some sort of virtual document distribution system. You can't just be handing out binders and paper copies, as might happen at an in-person meeting. Your distribution approach could be something as basic as giving all members access to Dropbox or a smart portal designed specifically for board meetings. Some organizations will also require translation services.

The other technology you need is a virtual meeting platform. One example that many people are familiar with is Zoom. If you already know how Zoom works because you are using it for other purposes, it may be appropriate for your AGM. One factor that will influence your choice of platform is the number of people expected at the meeting. And keep in mind that virtual meetings are better attended than in-person ones. Zoom had some very public issues with security during the early months of COVID, but those are now resolved. So, if you're comfortable with the level of security it offers, go for it. Zoom can host very large groups, and it's easy to use.

Another option is Webex from Cisco. They've been in the business of secure communications for a long time. The user interface may be a challenge, though, for people less familiar with technology.

And there are other options such as GoToWebinar and GoToMeeting. The GoTo family is less secure than Webex but can also host large numbers. Adobe Connect has some fun voting features but is relatively expensive. Like Microsoft Teams, it may not be appropriate for large numbers of participants.

The platforms mentioned above are the main ones we see companies using.

Security and meeting size are the two dominant criteria for choosing a platform. Additionally, some organizations want the capability to rebroadcast the virtual meeting. This could be accomplished with a rebroadcast system on top of your actual virtual meeting system. You need to ensure your service can handle that. Also, in this case, the audience would not have direct communication access.

Whichever platform is selected, the key is to practice! Make sure everyone involved in making your meeting a success is hands-on familiar with your choice and also the features required. Someone who is familiar with Zoom for chatting with family will need to be familiar with how to use some of Zoom's more advanced features for an AGM.

You should have a practice session before your AGM. That's also where you learn the limits of your selected technology. Learning this at the AGM is not fun. The practice session is also where participants learn their roles. These too may be different or modified from an in-person meeting. For instance, you can't do a roll-call with eight hundred people. You need to find an alternative.

With potentially different rules, roles, and technologies in play, you need to practice.

And have patience. Everyone is trying to do the best within the limitations of the platform. And every platform is a little bit different. Some are better than others or have different features. Pick the one that'll work best for your needs and budget.

Special Rules

More people attend a virtual AGM. This means everything takes a bit longer. To deal with this, you will need to limit speakers' time and candidates' campaign time to something less than you would for an in-person meeting.

Another consideration is the chat function. Different organizations use the chat function for different purposes. It may be best to disable the chat function during an AGM. Enable it at the beginning and during the breaks for use as a socializing function and also as a way to ask for help if you need tech support, although everybody should have a private way to connect with the IT support person. But if you leave the chat window live during a virtual AGM, everybody sees a distracting and potentially irrelevant sidebar conversation.

When people use chat to propose amendments, to vote, or to put forth interjections such as, "I'm trying to get the chair's attention," or "Don't vote for him," and "I have a better amendment," it gets so noisy and confusing! The chair, in particular, will need to decide whether to ignore or pay attention to the chat. If the chair pays attention to it, then it's like the tail wagging the dog. Special rules for holding a virtual AGM may want to touch on questions like how to use chat. Another option is making the chat function visible only during the meeting to the team, the chair, and their support team in order to protect it from misuse.

Two of the most challenging aspects of a virtual AGM are credentialing and the elections. Credentialing is an administrative challenge because there are a lot of people that you need to vet in a short space of time to get them in. And you need to ensure that only people who have the right to vote are voting. The election is challenging because it's not something that you can do just by a simple hand poll. These are the types of issues for which a special rule for a virtual AGM can be considered.

Agenda Development

First, ensure that everything that must be put before your shareholders or members—what you're mandated to deal with at an AGM—is on the agenda. Try to keep the agenda as simple and streamlined as possible. Anticipate points of contention or questions and proactively address them in your agenda planning and presentation.

Keep it Simple

Certain topics must be covered at an AGM. But a virtual meeting is new ground and it would be wise to remove from the agenda anything that doesn't need to be there. Keep it simple. You need the chair's report, and you need the CEO's report. The financial statements are required as is the appointment of auditors. If you typically have committees report to the AGM, one suggestion is to provide the committee reports but limit the allotted time for Q&A to even as little as ten minutes. The reports are for information and there are no motions. Keep it short.

Prerecord any planned presentations and stream them at the appropriate time from a place that has the most stable and fastest internet. This solves a couple of problems. First, it keeps the messages to the allotted time. You will find that the key messages are clearer as a result. And should the chair or CEO lose internet connection, their message is prerecorded so you won't miss a beat.

If possible, avoid bringing anything highly controversial to your first virtual AGM. You already have a lot that is new in this process. Keep it basic. At an AGM, you're enabling legislation. Now, it varies from sector to sector and region to region, but there are always things that must go back to your shareholders or your members to decide, for instance, an appointment of auditors, the election of officers and directors, and presenting your financials and year-end report.

It is important to note that bylaws can't take anything away from what the act requires you to bring back to your AGM. But they can add, meaning you can delegate more authority to your members or your shareholders than the act requires. A lot of organizations do that.

Check your bylaws to confirm what you promise. What's your agreement with your members or your shareholders about what you will bring to them? That's your basic starting point; that's what you absolutely must bring forward. You also may even have a policy for that agreement, which is a little easier to change if you must.

Anywhere you make changes, you also have to communicate why you would make a change and why you would not be bringing something forward. You want to simplify for your virtual AGM and communicate to your shareholders and members why you are doing so by telling them something like this: "It's a virtual AGM because of extraordinary circumstances. We're all trying to get through this together. We're going to make this meeting as simple as possible." If you normally have a verbal report that goes along with the committee report and you're not doing that in your virtual meeting, explain this to your membership and tell them the reason for the change. Assure them that you want feedback and questions and have made time for that, but make it clear that nobody is going to read the report aloud.

Time It

It is important to have time for your agenda. Everything takes a bit longer in a virtual meeting. People may forget or not know how to take their mute off, for example. Technical issues can slow your meeting.

Don't forget in your agenda planning to schedule breaks! People need to stretch and replenish. A virtual meeting is a different physical and mental experience, and it can be more tiring than anticipated.

Do a walk-through rehearsal to test if the times allotted are reasonable. Make sure that you provide enough space and time for questions afterward.

Essentials Only

Always begin with the why. Why are you meeting? What are the necessary items?

You want to report on the past year, provide relevant material facts and disclosures, and answer questions around those topics. You want to allow shareholders and members to raise issues and ideas and to ask questions. You want to put forward the vision for the year ahead. You don't want to just be looking backward. You want to choose the new board members (If you do that within the AGM. Some organizations have a selection process for board members that is independent of the AGM). And you want to appoint your auditors.

Be an Assertive Chair

You may find that the chair needs to be more assertive in a virtual meeting. Don't be ambiguous. State at the start how much time you're going to spend on specific agenda items and emphasize that you can't spend more if you expect to get to all the other things that you need to do, including hearing from attendees. You're essentially negotiating a covenant at the beginning of the AGM.

Some software options allow you to have a timer on the side of the screen, visible to all. Some people might find that stressful, but it can be a helpful reminder. At the least, the chair needs to be cognizant of time.

Be prepared for questions and dissent, and build that into your meeting time. You need to be realistic about this because in an emergency, with disruption to business, there will be questions about dealing with the human and financial effects of the emergency. What has the emergency forced you to go through as an organization? And how are you dealing with that? What are the contingency plans, and what is the plan for business continuity? What is your recovery plan?

In most cases, the CEO's report and the Q&A around that happen early in the AGM before you get to financial and other reports and your auditor's appointment. It will likely take longer and needs to be well-planned.

Remember, consider having your reports prerecorded. This can go beyond the CEO's report to the auditor's report, and in member-based elected boards, the campaign presentations from each of the candidates nominated for the board. These reports can all be prerecorded.

Team

Chairing a virtual AGM is challenging. All the things that happen at an in-person AGM are going on, and on top of that is the complexity added when the AGM is done virtually. Have key team members available to support the chair, both in preparation planning for a successful virtual AGM and during the meeting itself.

Team Roles

The key is to have a process to manage the functions of a virtual meeting. Everyone on the team has their responsibilities, such as registration or chat room management. And even when those functions are the same as at an in-person meeting, the virtual setting may require a different skill set to manage that function than an in-person meeting requires.

For example, the person who does registration at an in-person meeting enjoys greeting people, pointing attendees to the coffee room or the coat check, and checking a printed member list. But in a virtual situation, that person needs to be quick at navigating an electronic member list in order to rapidly verify people and usher them into the virtual meeting room.

It's important in any meeting to verify who's in the room and who can vote. But in a virtual setting, if someone is phoning in, the chair might only see the phone number. The question then is, how do you verify if that is someone who should be in the meeting or if they are eligible to vote? A system and a person responsible for that verification are essential in a virtual meeting.

Technology

The other huge component of a virtual meeting is technology. At an in-person meeting, the technology used is less robust. For a virtual meeting, there may be several different software platforms in use. This means that tech support will require a team, including people who can take phone calls and emails from attendees who can't figure out how to get into the technology or can't sign in. You need someone tech-savvy to manage that front-end customer service role just to make sure everybody that should get in does so.

In many regions the internet is not fiber-optic fast. People filling the virtual roles must have adequate internet to accomplish their tasks. They may have the tech knowledge, but they also need reliably fast connectivity to accomplish the role assigned.

Physical Space

One's physical space—what participants see when one is on video—can also be an issue. Family photos or macramé ducks in attendees' backdrops aren't terribly problematic, but inappropriate, distracting, or political material should be avoided. And then there's cats and kids. It's best to have a private, secure, and neutral physical space from which to work.

If possible, have the chair and maybe the two or three core members of the team physically together in the corporate boardroom, and have your IT staff there, too. The technology will be better than your iPad from home. The only caveat is to ensure everybody respects the public health advisories on physical distancing. You will want to follow all recommended health protocols in your jurisdiction to ensure everyone's safety. It is probably a good idea for the chair, the secretary, the IT support, and maybe the parliamentarian to be in the same room if you can do so safely. For sure, it reduces the complexity of the connectivity among your team and also the risk of technology not working.

Practice

You've got to practice. You've got to do a run-through with everyone on the team. The active members of the team especially need to understand the technology, most specifically, the part of the technology they're using and perhaps even an alternative to it. For example, if you are anticipating using the hands-up function and it's not working, you need to have a Plan B. Making a plan and running through it will help to define your agenda, timing, and rules of order. A trial run will also help you identify where any of those pieces need to be tweaked for a virtual event.

In a virtual meeting, the chair will need someone, typically the secretariat, to help with motions and amendments and make sure that participants are clear about what it is they're voting on. This person would clarify what's been decided and record the results of motions and decisions in the meeting minutes. It's also a good plan to have two scrutineers. Your legal counsel and the chair of your nominating committee are the two most likely people to fill that role.

It's not the chair's job but the team's job to ensure voting is conducted in an orderly and independent fashion and that the results are compiled and delivered back to the chair.

Consider using closed captioning. There is software available that will do closed captioning in real time, showing what the chair is saying and displaying the verbal reports. It provides a secondary method for participants to receive information.

The chair is like the conductor of the orchestra. Typically, the chair is not the person who answers most of the questions that are raised in an AGM. Instead, the chair will direct those questions to the appropriate person, for example, "That's a question for the audit committee chair," or "That's a question for the governance committee chair." You need to ensure, in your rehearsals, that these people understand that such directives may be coming, and they need to be ready and able to respond.

Registration and Credentialing Voting Members

Registration can be hectic, with everyone arriving, virtually, at the same time. It's helpful to have a platform that allows everybody to come into a waiting room or a green room and then be able to credential them. Again, have people here who are agile on the keyboard to quickly get those people credentialed and moved into the meeting room. You need to ensure that you have allotted enough time and resources to complete the registration process in a timely way. That includes having a process in place to verify who's in the room and what their voting status is. You must ensure that only registered members or shareholders are included in your voting.

You need to have a quorum and to be able to verify that by knowing not just how many people are in the room but how many registered members or shareholders are in the room. Your technology may make this easier, but you'll need to know how you'll handle the situation if you do not have quorum. For instance, larger companies are hiring organizations like Broadridge or Lumi to run their AGMs and to affirm the registration of attendees and shareholders, their voting status, and their access to communications.

How many shares a particular shareholder has will determine how much voting status they have. It's weighted voting. These companies use technology to ratify shareholder status because they may have hundreds of people listening in, and it would be virtually impossible to put all shareholders through a waiting room. Consider your scale. And look to approaches, perhaps even customized ones, that can automate verification for you.

Pre-registration

If you expected even a hundred people at an AGM, and if you had to put them all through a waiting room to verify their status, how long would it take per person to do that? And then how far ahead of time would you need to start your registration process? No one wants to sign in an hour in advance. And then at one minute to three o'clock, you'd have seventy people sitting in a waiting room waiting to be registered. That's just going to back you up. How you're going to do this, how you can automate it, who the right team members are, and how they are going to make that happen are all critical considerations.

Have a pre-registration room. You want the meeting to start on time, and you don't want to be checking people in when the meeting is supposed to start. Remember, the person who does registration at in-person meetings may not have the skill set required to do virtual meeting registration. Adapt.

A system such as Zoom or Webex is going to allow only registered users into a room. To give your pre-registration room a fighting chance of qualifying those people, ensure each has a valid email address that's connected to an account they have access to. It is the simplest way to ensure that your security person at the virtual door can verify the participant is who they say they are.

Pre-registration is great, but you do need to understand how it's applied. How does it get used or linked on the day of the meeting? You need the right technology for pre-registration to be scrutiny-proof. You can't necessarily do that with Zoom, for instance, without having a human to verify attendees' identities.

Motions and Amendments

There will be some standard motions at your meeting, such as approval of the agenda and appointment of the auditor. It's easy to have those on the screen. Someone should be tasked with the jobs of sharing these on the screen and making any amendments to the text as needed. This requires working on the fly and the ability to process motions properly.

Do You Need a Parliamentarian?

The chair, too, needs expertise, and not simply with the technology. For example, if a motion is put forward and then somebody amends it, does the chair know to not call for a vote on the main motion as amended without first voting on the amendment?

Not every chair is familiar with processing motions and following the rules of orders. Some boards are small and don't need to use *Robert's Rules of Orders* to work effectively together. In these cases, a chair might only use those rules once a year: at the AGM. Someone needs to understand the rules of order, and if it's not the chair, then someone else needs to support the chair on this, such as a parliamentarian.

The chair and their support person require a private communication channel, for instance, a private chat function or a phone line to the chair. This way, if the chair has an issue, they can talk privately with their support person. In an in-person meeting, the support person might sit beside the chair, and then the chair can lean in and whisper. In a virtual meeting, the parliamentarian might have the right to unmute and suggest a private phone call. For instance, they may interject with, "Madam Chair, we may want to discuss this," and then get on a phone call with the chair. You don't want to have that conversation in front of the entire assembly because that can become chaotic. You don't want input from the armchair-rules expert in the crowd. And you don't want to use rules like a cudgel rather than like a walking stick to help navigate working together.

You may need an expert parliamentarian to assist the chair. It's a question of risk. The degree of formality of legal rules is going to depend on the risk in your organization of things going off-track and being challenged and grinding your AGM to a halt.

If there's not much risk of that, you can follow a fair amount of common sense when it comes to votes, motions, and amendments. But depending on the experience of the chair, the complexity of the agenda, and the number of people in attendance, you may benefit from having an expert at the ready. Your corporate secretary or legal counsel might be in this role in lieu of a parliamentarian.

A parliamentarian could be appointed as the presiding officer of your AGM.

Interrupting Motion

An interrupting motion gives a participant the right to interrupt wherever you are in the agenda. You might be in the middle of discussing an amendment or discussing another motion or a report. These interrupting motions take priority.

If you follow *Robert's Rules of Order*, for instance, an interrupting motion might be a point of order or point of privilege. In an in-person meeting, a participant could simply say, "Madam Chair, I have a point of privilege." This interrupts whatever else is going on. In a virtual meeting, the question is, how can a participant interrupt? If someone raises their hand, they'll just go on a speakers' list. One way is to have a separate Q&A pod that's designated just for that purpose. If somebody needs to interrupt, then they type their question or comment in this designated space.

The most effective way to do this is not to type out the whole point of order. Instead, simply type, "point of order." Again, there needs to be someone designated to monitor that pod and who also has the privilege to unmute to say, "Madam Chair, there's a point of order." Then, the chair could deal with it just as they would in an in-person meeting by commenting, "Please state your point of order..." and going through that.

Enabling Debate

You want an AGM that empowers democracy. Decision-making is not the whole point of it. To the extent you can, you want to make sure that all the substantive, dissenting views are heard. Of course, that doesn't mean that every shareholder or member needs the right to speak to every motion. The chairs can exercise discretion in the moment. For instance, if you hear similar dissent three, four, five times, exercise discretion and say, "Let's give this two more minutes, and then we'll move on." If anyone has something new to say, they can say it, but there's no need to keep repeating points that have already been made. This might be preferable to having arbitrary limits on the time allotted or the number of questions allowed.

There needs to be a balance between respecting everyone's time and respecting the democratic process. The chair needs to have the ability to read the room, even if it's virtual. Is there a major point of dissent that needs more discussion, or is there just repetition of what's already been said? You want to make sure that people feel heard and, as much as possible, mirror the sense of an in-person meeting in the virtual space.

Everything is timed. Your agenda is timed, and you set a certain amount of time for discussion of a particular item. You set a time limit for how long individuals can talk. This means they must make their point clearly and quickly. If you have a rule that says a person can have one rebuttal and you have a speakers' list with a speakers' order, then you must follow the rules.

Recognizing Speakers

An orderly, consistent, and fair process needs to be in place to recognize speakers.

In most cases, you're going to use your usual rules of order and, if necessary, the special rules that you put in place for a virtual AGM. The purpose of rules of order is to provide an orderly process to permit decisions to be made by a majority while giving voice to minority views, allowing them an opportunity to persuade the majority to shift their perspective. That's democracy.

You do want to strictly follow the rules of order when you're dealing with a virtual AGM. Keep to the rules about motions, amendments, and speaking order. Adhere to time limits for speaking, allowing people to only speak to one motion and with a time limit of two minutes, for example. Set limits for questions on open motions. If there are any changes to your rules of order or if special rules are in place for a virtual meeting, you must communicate those to members before the meeting.

The key to chairing is consistency. Be clear in advance what the rules are, and then follow and enforce those rules. Make sure you are being fair in hearing minority views. But once you've heard the minority views, don't be afraid to go ahead and call for the vote. Let the majority decide, and then move on to the next agenda item.

To mirror an in-person meeting, you want your virtual meeting attendees to have an opportunity to be recognized to speak. At the same time, you don't want anyone to dominate the conversation, so have an orderly, consistent pattern. As at an in-person meeting, participants want an opportunity to influence people and have the right to try to do so.

How do you recognize speakers, and how much time do you give them? These aspects of your virtual meeting may be different from your in-person meeting rules. At an in-person meeting, participants might go to a microphone in the audience. It's difficult in a virtual meeting to say one person has access to the microphone and another person doesn't. With a small group of a dozen or so, it might be possible to manage by having people raise their hands on video to join a speakers' list. But that would not be manageable with a large group.

You might decide it is more efficient to use the *hands-up* feature of your virtual platform to recognize speakers.

A Word About Chat

The chair has a lot of balls to juggle—paying attention to the agenda, paying attention to who is speaking, plus trying to pay attention to a chat room where people are asking questions. And what about someone who wants to speak? Should there be a first-time speakers' list? And who gets priority when someone wants to speak a second time? There needs to be someone other than the chair tasked with managing the chat. This person could have the ability to interrupt and the ability to say, for example, "Madam Chair, so-and-so is wishing to speak. This person has not had an opportunity to speak. This is their first time speaking."

Using a chat room can be problematic because it can be misused, or it can simply be a distraction that can take you down some rabbit holes. Problems arise when people use the chat function literally to chat: "How's the weather?" "How are you doing?" This would rarely happen in an in-person meeting, but it does tend to happen in a virtual meeting when a chat feature is available to everyone.

If your technology does not have polling, you don't have a hands-up feature, or the chat tool is the only way you've got to register questions and votes, then you'll need to have chat turned on. And you'll need to have someone dedicated to monitoring it.

People are sometimes under the mistaken impression, especially in Zoom meetings, that chat is private if it is sent from one user to another. This is only partly true. For example, if John sends a message to Sue, maybe a catty comment about the chair's new hairstyle, then that message is private during the session; it is one-on-one communication. But the administrator of that session may have the ability afterward to go into the chat log and view all messages, including what was thought to be a private communication between two users in that chat.

Voting and Elections

An AGM is where an organization makes decisions. To do that, attendees need to be able to vote.

One member = one vote is a more complicated process in a virtual setting. When you have proxies and weighted voting along with that, it creates more layers of complexity. There may be limitations to whatever platform you choose. For a vote that simply requires a majority, such as an agenda, it can be quicker for the chair to simply ask about objections. For instance, if an attendee wants to put forward a motion for a recess and states, "Madam Chair, I move to recess for five minutes," rather than going through the whole process of hands-up or taking a poll, the chair could simply say, "Is there any objection to having a five-minute recess?" And if there are no objections, a declaration, "We'll have a five-minute recess," can be made. This can speed up the process and is very much the same as an in-person meeting.

If something's a little more complicated and you do need to vote, with a small enough group, you may ask people in favour to simply raise their hands. Again, this is not going to work well with large groups. Many platforms have agree/disagree buttons that can be used if this process is agreed upon in advance.

The hands-up feature is great for a straightforward vote. For example, if it's a simple 50 percent majority vote that doesn't need to be anonymous and is something that you would raise hands for at an in-person meeting, using the hands-up tool is a quick and easy way for attendees to vote.

Depending on the technology you use, there are several ways to do simple voting. You just need to understand what options the technology provides and have in place a process and a person who understands that technology—someone to count those votes and provide the results in a timely fashion.

People attending the AGM need to know how the technology works. Certainly, before the meeting, they should be instructed on how voting happens. For example, if they're supposed to put their hand up, they need to know where to find that button on the screen and how it works. It is useful for participants to be able to look at the software program beforehand and practice using it. You don't want the vote to go on and on as people fumble with the system, and you don't want people to not be able to vote simply because they can't figure out the technology.

A system such as Broadridge, for example, can do registration, and it has a robust voting platform built in. If you have the budget, systems like this are an excellent choice. When you get into proxy voting, for example, the process can get complicated and require more than a show of hands. ElectionBuddy is a software that allows for options such as weighted voting. There are other options as well.

If there is any level of complexity with your voting, you're going to want to make sure that you have some sort of audit trail. Many election systems have a robust audit trail. Be sure to do your research.

If a participant does not have an internet connection, they can't raise their hand or contribute to a chat. But they can still vote by phone. You are going to need to ask for that person to vote verbally. Many election software systems are useful for verifying a voter's identity. They can confirm that the phone number the voter is calling from is indeed that of a qualified voter.

Keep your shareholder and member contact information current. Ultimately, any system for voting is going to require that you have clean, up-to-date member lists, with the right email addresses and cell phone numbers, if those are being used. If you don't have a clean list, you're not going to be confident that the right people are in the virtual room.

The same is true for auditing. The whole point of auditing is to make sure that everyone is assured that the election process is secure and fair. And one way that happens is by ensuring up-to-date contact information. If somebody gets left off that text list and doesn't get the opportunity to vote, or you have an old cell phone number on file, they don't want to hear, "Hey, we sent it to you." They want the opportunity to vote, to be heard.

Elections

Most AGMs have elections of some sort, either for officers or board members. And there are elections with balloting or secret voting. Not all platforms give you the ability to do secret voting. An organization that requires this may have to hire a software company that has the skill set to do secret balloting. If yours is a small organization that doesn't have the financial ability to be able to hire somebody to do that, another option is to have your legal counsel act as the scrutineer. In that way, people can call in their votes to a person who is bound by confidentiality. The scrutineer is not allowed to give out information on who voted or how, and then when they're asked to destroy the ballots, they destroy them. Depending on the size of your group, your legal counsel may need help. It comes down to trust.

Proxies and Weighted Ballots

If your elections require a simple yes or no vote or a choice among three things, you can do a poll or use the agree/ disagree function. Zoom has a polling function that allows you to vote that way. You can probably deal with almost all of your votes this way. You can set up a process with your scrutineers where voters can email, text, phone, or use some combination of communicating your secret ballot through to the scrutineers. The scrutineers have an oath of confidentiality. They compile the results. They report the election results back.

Understand what is called for in your bylaws. For instance, if proxy voting is in the bylaws, you need to have a process beyond a show of hands to handle that. A small group may be able to handle this manually. But a good choice of technology—and some are not expensive—solves a lot of issues with both voting and registration.

There are other options for secret ballot voting, particularly with proxy voting, voting offline, and voting through the mail. Some organizations choose to separate the election and proxy voting from the virtual AGM and deal with it separately.

Observers

Some organizations are required to allow nonvoting observers. You may consider live-streaming the meeting for that audience, which adds yet another layer of technology.

If you have the budget for it, you can add this third platform layer. Lumi or other similar dedicated technology can completely manage the voting side of your meeting. There is a risk of somebody challenging the vote, which may cause your organization to get bogged down in legalities around the voting. Another option is to allow only your voting members into the meeting and to have nonvoting observers join through the live-stream broadcast. This latter option is manageable and is probably the simplest solution.

Some organizations have chosen to open the meeting to both voting members and nonvoting observers, which is what you would probably do if you were mirroring an in-person AGM. In that case, you need to ensure you've preregistered the voting members. Then, you can identify which of the people in the room are eligible to vote. The size of your meeting may decide this because if there are eight hundred people in the room, that's going to be almost impossible, but if there are only eighty to ninety people, the scrutineers, or whoever is responsible for managing the voting process, can do it. With a smaller number of participants, you want to have them preregistered or pre-credentialed, or have them go through some type of process to allow only the eligible to vote.

CHAPTER 4
CHAIRING A VIRTUAL MEETING

Boards have to rapidly adapt to meeting virtually, and this provides many challenges. Right from the start, there is the question of whether it's even legal for your organization to hold virtual meetings. Then, your organization needs to select the technology to facilitate a virtual meeting and get your team up to speed on using it. There are security issues, different from those at an in-person meeting, in addition to the basic meeting management procedures and tools that may need to be revised for a virtual setting. It is more challenging to keep people engaged and ensure substantive dialogue and debate on the significant issues in a virtual meeting.

Virtual Is Different

For most organizations, virtual meetings are a new phenomenon. Without good preparation and facility with the technology, too much time can be wasted at the beginning of the meeting just trying to get people settled in and comfortable with the technology. As much as any AGM requires preplanning, some issues are specific to virtual meetings—issues such as chairs not knowing if the proper people are in the meeting, participants being unsure who is talking, or attendees being unable to get the chair's attention when they wish to speak. Too often there can be awkward silences, ambiguity, and confusion. A lack of familiarity with the technology or specific processes can cause virtual meetings to take much more time than in-person meetings. And more people will likely attend a virtual meeting than an in-person one.

It's a Real Meeting

For many, the virtual experience is thought of differently and perhaps not as seriously as an in-person meeting. People have a different attitude toward in-person meetings. In that situation, people expect a serious event. People arrive early, settle in, and maybe engage in a little social banter prior to the meeting starting. They turn off their phones, the meeting starts, and participants engage. There is debate; decisions are made. The agreements made are followed up, and participants respect the agenda and the allotted time.

But a virtual meeting is different. People just think about it differently. At an in-person meeting, you would never make a phone call in the middle of the meeting in the middle of the room. But in a virtual meeting that happens all the time. People put themselves on mute, turn off their video, and multitask, checking their email or social media. They even let the dog out!

Set the Ground Rules

You want your virtual board meeting to be a success and to do this, you need to set up the same expectations of a regular board meeting in the minds and the hearts of the meeting participants. That first hurdle is not an easy one because it requires you to help people think and feel differently about virtual meetings.

If you wouldn't expect it, do it, or tolerate it at an in-person meeting, the same is true for a virtual meeting. The chair needs to set the tone for this expectation and establish some ground rules that are going to help bring clarity and understanding around meeting protocol.

Virtual Protocols

Most people don't know this, but in Canada, your bylaws need to explicitly permit virtual meetings in order for you to hold them. This holds for three levels of meetings: shareholder or member meetings like an AGM; board meetings, whether they're regular or special meetings; and committee meetings.

Your organization's bylaws may not explicitly permit virtual meetings. But what most bylaws do permit is *partially virtual* meetings. This means some people are in a physical location holding an in-person meeting. Typically, that would be the chair, the CEO, the corporate secretary, and the technical support staff. And then your bylaws probably do permit board members to join that meeting using electronic means. Your bylaws are more likely to permit that than a fully virtual meeting. That's one way of making sure you're holding a legal meeting.

Governments

When COVID-19 emerged and organizations were forced to meet virtually, many did not have the legal right to do so. Most governments quickly stepped in and issued guidelines to assist boards to carry out their meetings even when in-person gatherings were prohibited. One of these guidelines states that you can change your bylaws, as a board, to permit virtual meetings. Some organizations have done this by passing the bylaw change as the first item of business, so that it becomes effective immediately, and then ratifying it at the next meeting. This way, you don't have to wait for member approval to hold a virtual meeting.

For example, in Canada, individual provinces declared states of emergency followed by issuing emergency regulation to permit any for-profit or not-for-profit corporation to hold virtual meetings of shareholders, members, boards, and committees. This regulation holds even if an organization's bylaws don't explicitly permit virtual meetings because it's an emergency ruling. Provinces also extended the timing of AGMs during the emergency. This enabled corporations to wait to hold them until ninety days after the emergency order was removed.

Board Level Policy

What legal expectations will be placed on participants in a virtual meeting? In the best scenario, your organization has an electronic meeting policy that the chair will be able to use to guide the management of the meeting and that the participants can also refer to.

Of course, many of the things that the chair is responsible for in virtual meeting management are the same that they would do in an in-person meeting. The number one tool in preparing for an effective board, shareholder, or committee meeting is the creation of the agenda and agenda management. And that's going to be particularly important for a virtual meeting.

Keep the Focus on Governing

First, ensure that time is allocated for substantive discussions about decisions on which the board needs to focus. There is a temptation in times of high risk, volatility, or change for the board to get caught up in operations and spend valuable board meeting time micro-managing or encroaching on management's job. Resist that temptation! Stay focused on oversight. Stay focused on direction monitoring and evaluation. In an emergency, you're going to allocate considerably more time for the CEO's report and a discussion around the CEO's report. And the CEO will want to sit down with the chair and agree on which parts of that report are for information, which parts are for discussion, and which parts are for decision.

Agenda Development

Following this, the chair will triage other agenda items to determine which of these are urgent and important enough to be included in the upcoming meeting of the board, which committee meetings should be going ahead, which items can be deferred, which can be bundled in a consent agenda, and which items can be tabled to a future meeting of the board or of the committee.

Once the agenda is finalized, you can establish your prereading packages and your information items for participants. Just like for an in-person meeting, those are sent as far in advance as possible to allow board members time to prepare.

Meeting Logistics

This is where it gets kind of tricky, especially if you're not wholly comfortable with technology. Just as in-person meetings have logistical needs, a virtual meeting has more. As you think about your technology choices, ask yourself, "Will everyone be able to access the technology?" "Will it support the work that we're trying to accomplish?" "Is it secure?" "Is it easy to use?" "Do we have appropriate technical support?" "Is it cost-effective?"

Board Portal

You will need at least two different types of technology functioning at the same time for a virtual meeting. The first is your board portal.

There are many board portals available, and different boards have different needs. But essentially, this important tool needs to ensure that the board documents are secure and kept confidential. It will also limit information access to only those people who are supposed to have access.

Some organizations use Dropbox for this purpose but for many reasons, it is not recommended. Instead, look at a smartboard portal like BoardConnex, a tremendous piece of software provided by Sandbox Software Solutions and Governance Solutions.

The other type of technology required is online meeting software. Some of these are Zoom, Webex, GoToMeeting, Google Meet, and Adobe Connect. There are many options and some are more secure than others. For security reasons, using Zoom for a confidential board meeting is not recommended. Adobe Connect is secure and has lots of add-ons for meetings. For instance, if you want to run a timer in the corner of your screen, you can buy an add-on for that, or if you want to allow people to raise their hands, there's an add-on for that. Adobe Connect can take and record virtual votes. For an AGM, that's a valuable feature. If your board is small, it may not be a worthwhile feature.

Consider your organization's needs and budget in selecting this necessary software, but this is not the board's job. It's a task that is normally done by management. Your job is just to make sure that you have these two pieces of secure technology in place and that you're comfortable they're secure and functioning well.

Audio-only

You can use audio-only for meetings. In some rural areas, for example, participants may not have the internet capacity to use video. Wherever possible, using both audio and video is best. You're going to get a much more dynamic meeting if you're using video. If you do use audio-only, there are fewer body language clues. In this case, it helps if speakers talk more slowly and don't forget to pause.

Technology Comfort

As the meeting chair, your new best friend is your tech support. It's ideal if they can be sitting next to you, at appropriate physical distancing. You want them there to make sure they can help you manage some of these things that are unique to virtual meetings and to help you monitor who's in the meeting.

But you can't expect tech support to manage a virtual meeting if none of your participants is familiar with the technology being used.

Don't wait to do that until the meeting starts. Nothing is more frustrating than planning for a meeting to start at nine and then spending until ten o'clock just getting people and their technology all working together. Your attack team should be working with each board member a day or two before the board meeting to make sure that everyone has access to the technological tools that you have in play.

Tech Support

Some organizations give board members iPads that are all set up for them. Other boards rely on participants to use their existing devices. Either way, you need to make sure participants know how to use them for the meeting. Do they know how to access the platform? Do they know how to sign in? Do they know their username and password? Is their hardware working? And does it interface with the technology being used for the meeting? Has it been tested? Do they know how to work their sound? Do they know how to work their video? Do they know how to use the chat? All of these questions should be resolved before the meeting, not during the first hour!

Some board members just need somebody to walk through the technology with them, to practice with them until it becomes easy for them. And your tech team can also create a simple, step-by-step guide for board members to follow. Anything you can do ahead of time will allow participants to hit the ground running and make for a much more effective meeting.

With all that is facing board members these days, meetings need to focus on the important decisions to be made. You need to keep your focus on the work of the board, not on learning to use your technology.

You want to make sure each of your board members has direct access to the tech team, for example, by email or cell phone text. You don't want them to interrupt the meeting with a technical issue, and you want to ensure any issues can be resolved quickly.

Encourage Early Arrival

Just as you would for an in-person meeting, ask participants to arrive fifteen minutes ahead of the virtual meeting. At an in-person meeting, people show up and they grab a coffee and maybe a little bite to eat. They socialize and they settle in. Set the expectation to do this at virtual meetings also. This is the time for participants to check their connections and make sure their audio is working, for instance. It also provides an opportunity to build some social rapport—even at a distance. Then, when you start the meeting, you start the meeting.

Confidentiality and Privacy

Virtual meetings are more susceptible to breaches of confidentiality and privacy than are in-person meetings. This is because your organization doesn't have control over the different locations from which participants are listening and watching the board meetings. Each participant in your meeting must know that it is their responsibility to manage their location to ensure that nobody else can hear what's taking place in the meeting. This holds whether they are joining the meeting from home, the office, or even the business center at the airport.

This adherence to strict privacy guidelines is part of your meeting protocol and something you, as the chair, need to remind participants about. At the beginning of every meeting, participants should be reminded that it is their responsibility to manage their personal space. It should be private. One device that is useful for this is a headset. It reduces the chance of other people accidentally hearing the confidential things that are being said in these meetings, and it improves the quality of audio, too.

Some organizations, even in the military and national security, understand that in the real world, spouses are an exceptional case, and it's not unusual for a board member to share confidential matters with a spouse. In this case, what sometimes happens is that the confidentiality policy extends to spouses, and spouses also need to sign a non-disclosure agreement.

Your board portal technology can also contribute to security. In some cases, the technology allows for the ability to assign security settings to individuals at the document level. Additionally, your online meeting software should be able to indicate who's in the meeting at any given time—when they sign in and when they sign out. That helps you manage a quorum and ensures that quorum continues during the meeting. In Zoom, for example, you can see who's on the call and who's not, although this is often indicated with a phone number rather than a name. In this case, you want to make sure your technical staff can match those phone numbers with names to know who's in the meeting.

In your meeting software, you should be able to track who's in a meeting. Your corporate secretary or assistant corporate secretary is going to be tracking that shareholders are the only ones in a meeting. If someone joins the meeting and you don't know who it is, you're going to challenge that person, whether they're on audio or video, and if they don't have bona fides, then you can remove them from the meeting.

Risk Management

One of the concerns with Zoom is that it doesn't have end-to-end encryption. For example, there was a concern that the British Cabinet was using it to meet and talk about national security questions. Probably the British Cabinet should not be using Zoom. For your board and committee meetings, it's a question of risk management and to what extent not having end-to-end encryption is a serious risk for your organization.

There were reports of Zoom issues where people were showing up in meetings who should not have been there (*meeting-bombing*) and also getting hold of email addresses of participants. Email is not a big issue; people can find your email address in many places. And the security issue around uninvited guests has been resolved.

In-Camera

If your technology is capable of identifying who's in the room at any given time, then you may be able to hold in-camera sessions using the same connection. Have the people leave who should not be there for the in-camera session. Those invited stay on the connection. This is not necessarily the best solution and it may not be foolproof. Instead, some clients create a second virtual meeting just for the in-camera session. Then, log-in information is provided only to the people who are included in the in-camera session or the executive portion of the meeting. This way you can be more confident that the in-camera session is not being encroached by people who shouldn't have access to it.

Participants

Who should be at your virtual meeting? It's easy in a virtual meeting to just add all kinds of people because you can, but it doesn't mean you should. Think about how adding people changes the dynamic of the meeting. Adding members of the management team or consultants, for instance, can affect the dynamic. You want your virtual meeting to, as much as possible, have the same dynamic as an in-person meeting. The more people that you add to your meeting, the more you dissipate the social cohesion of the board as a small group. For this reason, you may choose to limit the participation in a virtual board meeting to organization members, the CEO, and the corporate secretary. Then, those members of the management team who need to be there for a particular agenda item could rotate in and out of the meeting so that you can retain the dynamic of a socially cohesive small group. This is not a conference call that anybody can pop in and pop out of. Make sure that your meeting policy is in place and that participants are reminded of the process expectations upfront.

Keeping the group small, in the case of board or committee meetings for instance, also lets everybody see each other on-screen. Eighty percent of human communication is nonverbal, which is why it is so challenging to have any kind of substantive social cohesion and constructive engagement in telephone conference meetings. Having video with everybody able to see each other helps alleviate that challenge. Make sure that people know how and when to use the mute function, and discourage multitasking and other distractions. Being able to see each other helps keep people's attention on the meeting, too. And it is useful also to have people state their names each time they speak.

Open to the Public

Some board meetings, such as those held by school boards, need to have their meetings open to the public. The public may be prohibited from participating, but the meeting platform must allow the public to view the meeting. In this case, you want to make sure your technology enables their attendance. From a logistics point of view, you need to think about how you are going to get notice of the meeting out to the public and then have them log in. Then, you're going to hold the public portion of your meeting publicly and enable people to join. In many cases, these meetings allow the public to observe and then offer a time for members of the public to ask questions. You want to be able to enable that with your choice of meeting software.

Decisions

As chair, you'll want to think through each agenda item ahead of time. This is even more important for a virtual meeting. During the meeting, be prepared to bookend every agenda item succinctly and clearly. This means at the beginning of each agenda item you briefly and concisely frame the agenda items; this is what the board is being asked for. Then, at the end of every agenda item, before you move on, summarize the following: this is what we decided; this is what the next steps are; this is what you can expect; this is what we agreed upon.

Email Voting

Email voting is a little different than electronic voting. The main issue with email voting is you have to have unanimous consent on a motion because the organization is not meeting with due notice and a proper forum. On the other hand, electronic voting takes place in a legal meeting with due notice and quorum. All you need is a majority for an electronic vote to pass.

Maintaining Focus

Especially at times like these, it's easy for a board to get drawn into the weeds rather than focusing on strategy and risk and oversight. A meeting between the chair and CEO ahead of the board meeting is even more critically important for a virtual meeting to ensure the chair is clear on what the CEO needs from the board ahead of the meeting. Then, as the chair, you need to continue to guide and nudge people in that direction. Your skills as a facilitator are going to be tested in a virtual meeting!

Another tool in your toolkit as a chair is to specifically call on people for their input or questions. In a virtual meeting, you're probably going to have to do that more intentionally—more consciously—than at an in-person meeting. For example, just going around the table from time to time, checking in, and having people share what they're thinking will help them stay engaged and draw out the silent board members. Another option is to preassign tasks.

Engagement

Some of the most uncomfortable moments in virtual meetings are those awkward silences. Certainly, in North America, we're not comfortable with silence. If left too long, it does become uncomfortable. And even during in-person meetings, if there's silence, somebody usually speaks up quickly to fill that silence. But sometimes silence is necessary. It's there to allow people to think. Sometimes silence means consensus and you can just move on, but sometimes it can mean the exact opposite. With an in-person meeting, body language often indicates what the silence means. But you need to be proactive with virtual meetings. As a chair, you want to make sure that you check in with board members to qualify the silence. If you think there is silence because everybody agrees, then confirm that. Ask, "Is everybody in agreement?" If you think the silence is because there's disagreement or confusion, ask if that's the case.

If the silence is because there is no consensus, people in the meeting can become uncomfortable. Don't just ignore it and go to the next item. As a chair, you need to break the silence, not by changing the subject but by calling out the reason for the silence and then working through the issue.

Engagement can be encouraged by the chair proactively calling on people. It is worthwhile for the chair to work their way around the room. You need to do this much more often in a virtual meeting than you do in a physical meeting because the conversation is much less dynamic and much less fluid. And get good at asking open-ended questions.

Nobody wants to be caught off guard. Let your board members know before the meeting that they're going to be in full view on video throughout the meeting and whether they will be called on specifically by you as the chair to speak at a particular agenda item point.

Keep in mind, people who dominate discussion in your in-person meetings are even more dominating in virtual meetings. Be prepared.

Get Visual

In the virtual meeting space, it is more needful than ever to get visual! Management presentations should be to the point with clear and meaningful dashboards. Enterprise-wide dashboards that provide a 360-degree view on what's happening in and around the organization and that go beyond historical results to highlight clear trends should be the order of the day. Don't just tell the board what's happening; show them.

Minute-taking

There are four key matters the chair should be thinking about in terms of minutes: clarity, accuracy, security, and liability.

Clarity

Taking minutes in a virtual meeting is in many ways no different from an in-person meeting. But it can be more challenging for the recording secretary, the person taking the minutes. As chair, you want to be sensitive to this. It helps if the chair and secretary are in the same room. But either way, you want to make sure there is clear communication between the chair and the secretary. One simple step that can assist this is having the secretary write out motions so they can be displayed on the screen.

Accuracy

You display the motion so that everybody around the board-room table, or the shareholders and members, are clear about what is being voting on. The same need for clarity applies to seconding a motion. Encourage people to say, for example, "I'm Peter Smith; I'm going to move this motion." "I'm Beth Evans; I second this." This process is helpful to the recording secretary who may not know everybody's voice.

Security and Liability

The recording secretary will probably record the virtual meeting to prepare the minutes. This doesn't mean that your minutes are a transcript. That would be messy. Your minutes should be a summary of the key decisions and the substantive due diligence that the board goes through, just as they would be for an in-person meeting. The key here is that once the minutes have been approved at the next meeting, go back and make sure that all recordings are destroyed, just as you would destroy any notes or any drafts of minutes.

Anybody can record a meeting. Anybody can cut and paste items from a virtual meeting with what they can get on their computers. Make sure your meeting policy is clear about this: participants will not record any portion of the meeting. You can't have direct control over this, so the onus is on participants to comply. If somebody does copy the chat window or record a meeting, these files are discoverable in litigation, which raises the issue of what you could unintentionally be liable for. The chat function in particular is a component that can be abused or misused by board members during a meeting.

The purpose of the chat function during a meeting is to have an offline conversation that you need to have at a particular moment. One common example is if you're having a technical issue and you need to communicate with your support people without interrupting the meeting. After the meeting, ensure that the chat window contents are deleted and every participant also deletes it. Chat conversations should not form a part of anybody's record. The chat window content does not become part of the official minutes.

Sometimes participants want to use the chat window to ask questions. This is a practice that should be discouraged. If a participant has a question, they should ask the question. You don't want a chat to become part of your minutes.

AFTERWORD

This book began by claiming meetings are central to life and business. The dialogue, debate, and decisions that take place in meetings are what create change and drive innovation and growth, both personally and corporately. That's why we meet.

Since the onset of the COVID-19 pandemic, there has been considerable learning in the *how to* of virtual meetings, which allows significant opportunity for deep levels of decision-making toward real change, innovation, and growth.

What We Have Learned

- **Have all hands on deck.** In the virtual environment, meeting management is accentuated. Therefore, make sure you have all hands on deck to ensure the meetings run seamlessly.

- **Be prepared.** The technology and flow of your meeting will be under a microscope. The slightest glitch is highly noticeable. This means preparation is crucial.

- **Use good technology.** Technology that is easy to access and simple to use is fundamental to success. Throughout this book, we have mentioned several platforms and software solutions. We have used each of these to good effect, but there are many others. As you make your own choice, access and simplicity for the users should drive your decision.

- **Adapt the meeting to the environment.** Meetings need to be approached differently to meet the needs of meeting participants who gather in a different environment. You should not be married to how you have always done things. Match your approach to the meeting method and environment.

- **Break more frequently.** There need to be more frequent and regular breaks to enable clear thinking and focus. Virtual fatigue tires the brain, eyes, and our physical bodies. Regular breaks rest the brain and eyes and give us a little time to exercise our bodies, too. A brief break gives us time to think and process the content we have just met on and discussed. We come back to the conversation with fresh focus and clarity.

- **Be clear on the rules and expectations.** People will rise to the expectations that you place on them. Being clear on meeting rules and expectations not only makes for a smooth meeting, but it also protects the organization by providing clarity on the rules of engagement. We have included a sample Virtual and Electronic Meeting Policy in this book as a help for you in creating your own.

- **Chair with intention.** Leadership matters. The leadership of the chair of the meeting must be intentional. They must be focused and forceful while at the same time being facilitative and fast-paced.

- **Grow your audience and your engagement with them.** The online meeting environment has allowed us access to new audiences. People who otherwise could not attend a board meeting or annual general meeting can now join in from the comfort and safety of their own homes. Organizations are engaging more shareholders, members, and other stakeholders. AGM attendance is up. Engagement is up. This is good news for your organization.

Without a doubt, our greatest learning from this intense period of meeting online is this: done well and with intention, you can be *Virtually There!*

APPENDIX
SAMPLE VIRTUAL AND ELECTRONIC MEETING POLICY

Principle

The need for and advantages to holding virtual and electronic meetings from time to time are both acknowledged and necessary. This policy is intended to provide guidance for organizations when holding and participating in these meetings.

Policy

This policy provides for the use of virtual and electronic means for the holding of meetings of the members, board, and committees of a board, including a committee of the whole board.

Electronic meetings may be used to hold member, board, or committee meetings subject to due notice requirements for any such meeting being met (or waived by unanimous consent in special circumstances).

All participants must have access to the necessary equipment for participation. A right of membership is participation; therefore, the technology used must be accessible to all members who are included in the meeting.

All rules pertaining to in-person member, board, or committee meetings apply equally to electronic meetings, for example, notice, premeeting package requirements, quorum, minute-taking, voting, and confidentiality requirements.

All meeting participants must ensure they maintain complete privacy in their off-site meeting space. This will ensure all discussions are kept confidential and are only heard by those invited to and attending the meeting.

All provisions and policy related to in-camera meetings and conflict of interest will apply equally for electronic meetings of the members, board, or committees.

At no time will meeting participants record any portion of the meeting. The only exception to this is any recording made by the corporate secretary or other approved corporate officer for the purpose of minute-taking. Any such recording must be destroyed once the official minutes of the meeting have been approved.

In no circumstance are discussions in the chat function of virtual meeting software to be copied and saved by meeting participants or included as part of the official meeting minutes.

Subject to any conditions or limitations provided for under the act, regulations, bylaws, or this policy (which some jurisdictions waive during the course of a declared emergency), a member, board, or committee member who participates in a meeting through electronic means shall be deemed to be present at the meeting and will be recorded as in attendance at and part of the quorum of the meeting.

Virtual and Electronic Meeting Procedure

- The chair of the board or committee will be the chair of the meeting.

- Any technology employed will enable every participant to hear and be heard by all other participants in the meeting.

- The chair will ensure that declarations of conflict of interest are heard by all present and that those participating have an opportunity to verbally declare any conflict.

- The meeting will be administered in such a way that the rules governing conflict of interest are complied with.

- The electronic means will enable appropriate processes to ensure the security and confidentiality of proceedings, both regular and in-camera meetings. This may mean using separate connections and log-ins for scheduled in-camera/executive sessions.

- Attendance shall be taken and duly recorded to ensure participants are recognized as in attendance.

- Participants will identify themselves before speaking in order to assist the recording secretary in recording the minutes.

- Those participating in an electronic meeting shall notify the chair of their departure (either temporary or permanent) from the meeting, before absenting themselves, in order to ensure a quorum is maintained.

- All meeting participants must have a copy of the meeting package, including the agenda, prior to the meeting for reference during the electronic meeting.

- Wherever possible, motions coming forward at the electronic meeting should be prepared ahead of the meeting with one of the eligible members indicating their willingness to let their name stand as mover and another as seconder. Prior to the vote, the chair will read each motion and indicate the member who is moving and seconding the motion.

- Voting at electronic meetings shall be carried out as follows to ensure that accurate records of votes are maintained:

  o When a vote is called, opposition to the motion is called first. If no one is opposed, the motion is considered carried.

  o If there is opposition, a show of hands (using either visual or technology tools) will be conducted, and the chair will announce whether the motion is carried.

  o The chair will make the decision as to whether the motion was carried or defeated.

  o If a recorded vote or a secret ballot is required, use the applicable technology to conduct this where available.

  o When the technology does not allow for those votes requiring a secret ballot, a confidential email should be in place between meeting participants and the scrutineer to facilitate secret votes.

- To avoid as much disruption as possible and to support seamless dialogue and debate, all participants will keep their electronic devices on mute unless speaking.

- Any open chat windows in the technology are to be used only to resolve technological problems—chat rooms should not be used for side discussions, lobbying other members and participants, or voicing support for motions on the floor. Members, boards, and committees meet and have authority only as a collective with due order.

Review: Annually by Governance and Nominating Committee

ABOUT THE AUTHORS

Dr. Debra L. Brown

- gained over thirty years' experience in corporate governance

- trained thousands of board members and C-suite executives

- consulted, coached, and mentored hundreds of boards

- co-created countless tools for boards to use—like BoardConnex, our smart board portal and our board and CEO evaluation tools

- co-authored *Governance Solutions: The Ultimate Guide to Competence and Confidence in the Boardroom* and *Governing in Scary Times: The Board's Roadmap for Governing Through and Beyond an Emergency*

- co-founded The Professional Director Education and Certification Program®

- holds a Professional Director Designation®

- authored and published dozens of governance articles internationally

- regularly contributes to *Ethical Boardroom*, a globally recognized corporate governance periodical

- holds a Doctorate in Leadership (Thesis: *Using Governance as a Tool to Transform Organizational Culture*)

Rob DeRooy

- gained over ten years' experience in corporate governance

- trained hundreds of board members and C-suite executives

- serves as faculty member of The Professional Director Education and Certification Program®

- teaches as faculty member of The Directors College

- holds a Professional Director Designation® and a Chartered Director designation

- held CEO position for an elevator manufacturing company

- has served on multiple boards of directors

Jake Skinner

- created innovative governance tools and solutions for over twenty years

- designed a comprehensive online school created to educate and certify Professional Directors®

- co-authored *The Governance Ideabook*, published by The Conference Board of Canada, as well as governance accountability benchmarking research reports and a major article, "The Seven Deadly Sins of Enron"

- co-created countless tools for boards to use—like BoardConnex, our smart board portal, and our board and CEO evaluation tools

ABOUT GOVERNANCE SOLUTIONS

As globally respected leaders in all things governance, we work with organizations and directors to unlock the full potential of their boards through our integrated portfolio of products and services. Our superior solutions offer everything you need to optimize your board.

governancesolutions.ca

OTHER BOOKS BY THE AUTHORS

Governance Solutions: The Ultimate Guide to
Competence and Confidence in the Boardroom

Today's board members need more tools, not more rules!

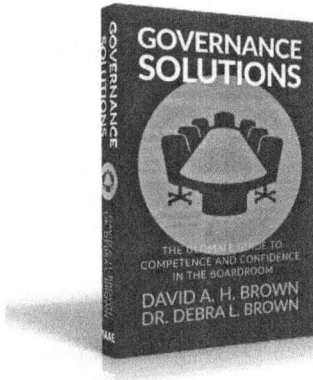

Governance Solutions: The Ultimate Guide to Competence and Confidence in the Boardroom is chock full of governance tools that make the complex seem simple and bring order to the chaos.

This is not just a book *about governance*; it tells you how to *do governance*.

Authors David A. H. Brown and Dr. Debra L. Brown deliver

- proven governance solutions: This book is a single source—the ultimate guide—for solving your governance problems.

- access: It includes almost seventy governance concepts and tools that are unique only to this book.

- competence and confidence: It covers the broad spectrum of governance issues from governance structure and process through boardroom leadership, culture, and behavior.

- answers! It tells you not only what works but just as importantly, what does not work in governance.

With so many spotlights trained on corporate boards, there could hardly be a better moment for hands-on, cutting-edge guidance on how directors can power success—and avoid traps. David and Debra Brown are world-class experts; their new book earns a place on director desks everywhere.

Stephen Davis, Ph.D.
Associate Director and Senior Fellow
Harvard Law School Programs on Corporate Governance and Institutional Investors

GOVERNING IN SCARY TIMES

COVID-19 threw the world into scary times!

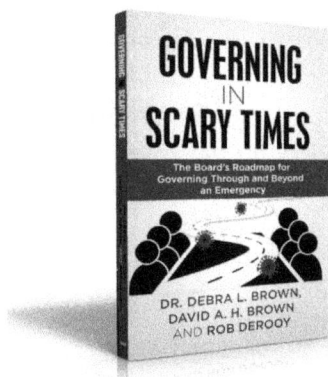

If the global pandemic taught us anything, it's that all organizations need a strategy to manage in a crisis. In *Governance in Scary Times*, authors Dr. Debra L. Brown, David A. H. Brown, and Rob DeRooy offer a step-by-step plan to prepare your board to provide direction for your company and reinforce your stakeholder confidence.

With a combined seventy-five years of experience governing companies and boards, the authors guide you through a process that will prepare you to answer key questions:

- Where are we headed?
- What obstacles and opportunities might we face along the way?
- Who will do what?
- What are the boundaries and guidelines?
- How will we resource our efforts?

Governing in Scary Times is your boardroom roadmap for navigating extreme challenges in your business. From developing a strategic plan to assessing risks and policies to getting and keeping the right people in place, the authors provide practical and proven advice that will equip your company to survive scary times—and come out stronger on the other side.

Another crisis is (always) coming. Use the strategies in *Governing in Scary Times* to ensure your organization is prepared.

EARN YOUR PROFESSIONAL DIRECTOR® DESIGNATION

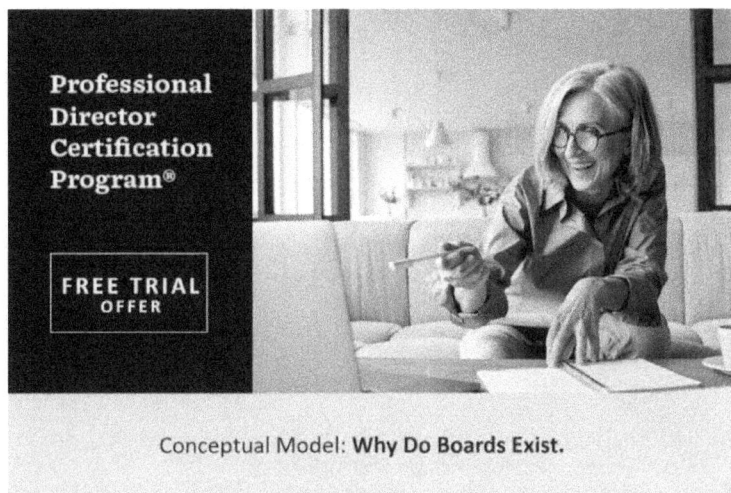